ANXIETY

ANXIETY

by

Bonnie Timmons

FAWCETT COLUMBINE · NEW YORK

To mom and dad
and the blackboard,
with love

ANXIETY

anx·i·e·ty (ăng-zī´ə-tē) n., pl. ~ties

1. A state of uneasiness and distress about future uncertainties; apprehension, worry.

ANXIETY

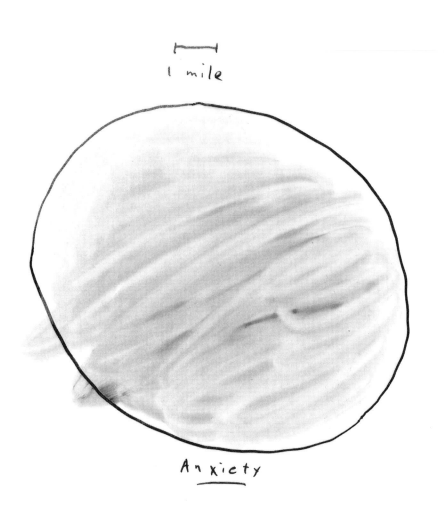

1 mile

Anxiety

you

How big it REALLY is

eyes that can SEE what's coming

you know what

brain (hard to see here) that KNOWS what's coming

wiggly lines around forehead →

← hair asunder

twitching lip muscles

← wiggily-drawn edges about the face

upper lip stuck to teeth

more wiggles

1. Facial give-aways

2. Body language

Tell-tale symptoms of ANXIETY

Mammograms

(HOLD STILL)

Germs before
vacation

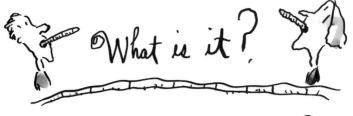

What is it?

Oh dear, this is it.
A BRAIN TUMOR!

Alas, my life
is over.

thump-
th-th-
th-thump

So young, so young...
But what is this—
a heart attack?

th-th-th-
th-th-
th-thump

Be still, my
beating heart, are
you failing me???

And this tingling in my arms. I must have multiple sclerosis!

But wait, hold it... that's melanoma.

CHOO

I knew I was sick

Nude sun bathing concerns

Gravity

1.

2.

Aging

Addiction

HOW TO QUIT!

Smoking

1. Smoke only those cigarettes you can balance on your nose.

2. Ask a close friend to keep your cigarettes from you.

3. Think of all the things you could be doing instead.

4. JUST QUIT

One bite too many

Going to the health club

Not feeling so good

CLAUStrophobia

clawstrophobia

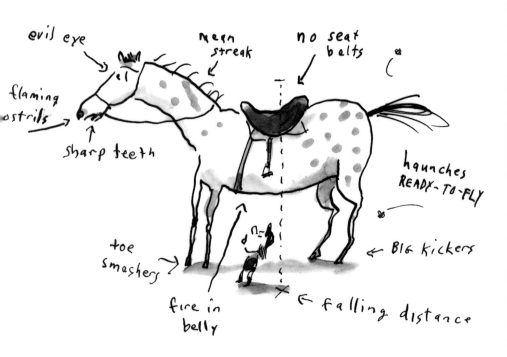

EQUIPHOBIA

Performance anxiety

Do I watch too much tv?

Dining alone

Is this my fourth or
fifth cup of coffee?

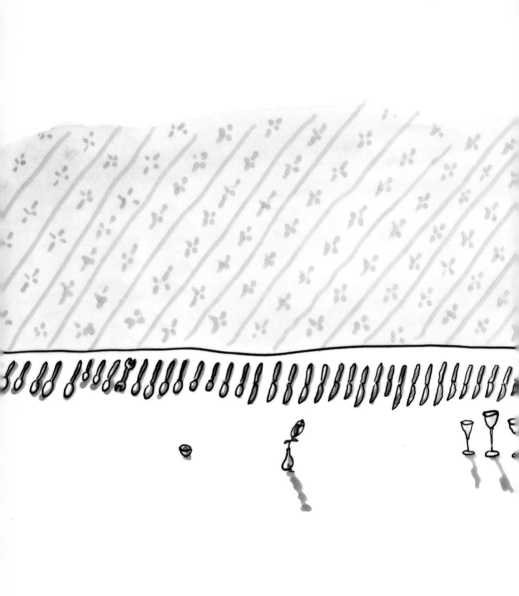

which fork do I use?

Exotic food

How do I look?

Before   After

Makeovers

Just a **TRIM**, PLEASE

voila!

Smart enough?

Tall enough?

Interesting enough?

Am I too trusting?

I DIDN'T DO IT

Seize the day! ☺

The FUTURE

Imperious sales ladies.

But do I REALLY NEED IT?

The greenhouse effect

Is it hopeless?

Deadline Anxiety

Can I write that novel?

That funny - LOUD - NOISE
in the basement
anxiety

I'm all alone ? ? ?

My shoelaces!

DON'T put me on hold

something's AMISS

Anxious Moments in dreamland

Forgot to check the brake

Forgot to attend math class all semester

Forgot to wear shirt and shoes to work

Forgot how to run

CONTROLING DREAMLAND ANXIETIES
a self-help guide to bedtime aerodynamics

Superman-Style

Hitchhiking

Breaststroke

Snorkeling

Rocket

Backstroke

Grounded

Flapping

Bouncing

Leaping steps

Astral Projection

Spinning liftoff

Failure to fly

Fear of women

Really really BAD
fear of women

Great expectations

Introducing him to your
friends

The RELATIONSHIP

Can it work?

OUR LOVE

Will it Last Forever?

The Sad Sad Tale of Betty and Tate

She found him at the Shop 'N Go. From the very start she knew he was special.

Betty and "Tate" went everywhere together.

They shared their innermost secrets

and created their own private world.

When "Tate" started bumping into things, Betty kissed his bruises

and fitted him with glasses

But when he began growing sprouts,

But THINK of all we had

yeeeech

Betty could no longer face her spud.

she ate him.

THE CHURCH

Drooling (then trying
to suck it back up)

Motherhood

Fatherhood

Although the delivery was normal enough, "Baby Tiny" seemed small and frail from the start.

None of the nice baby clothes fit,

And feeding was a big problem.

Within time she adjusted and discovered many helpful tricks.

But one day "Baby Tiny" got dropped,

And the rest is too gruesome to tell.

Parenthood

Finding the right neighborhood

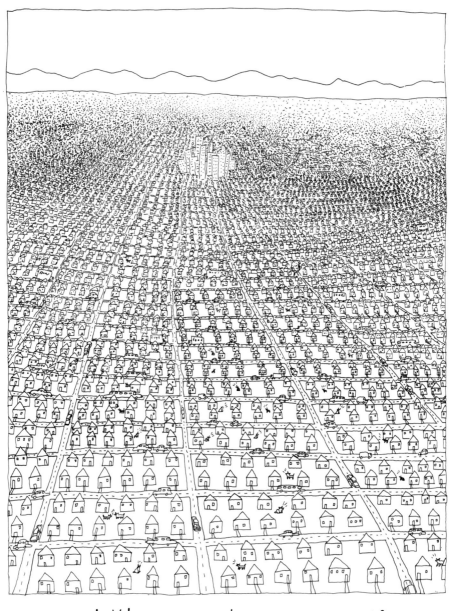

Will my new home say "me"?

should I ask for that raise?

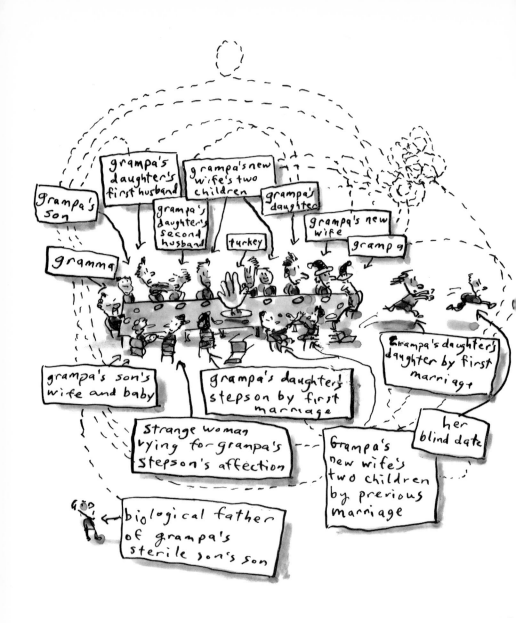

Family Reunion

what if I DON'T have kids?

Applying for a loan

First day on the job

Will they discover I'm REALLY
NOT QUALIFIED?

Flying Safe
A few tips on getting there
~Without Falling~

① Pack lightly and wear light-weight clothes. It is even advisable not to eat for 3 or 4 days before a flight. Every little bit of help you give your plane, the better.

② Remember: Not only are heavy metal objects NOT meant to fly, they can also be malevolent. ALWAYS bring a carrot or other treat for your carrier.

③ Take command of your destiny. Flap your wings. And not just when you happen to think of it — YOUR PLANE NEEDS YOUR HELP FULLTIME.

(don't forget to flap)

④ Don't read or listen to headphones and by all means, don't watch a movie during your flight. CONCENTRATE! If you are not paying attention, your plane may not be either.

⑤ Regardless of what the flight attendants say, DON'T stay in your seat while landing. Instead, JUMP as HIGH AS YOU CAN, PRECISELY when the plane touches down. The reasons for this are too technical to go into here. Just DO IT!

⑥ Most important of all, THANK the plane, sincerely. Give it a little pat or kiss on its wing tip when the flight is over and if you have, despite all the odds, landed safely.

Really enjoying those
once-in-a-lifetime
moments

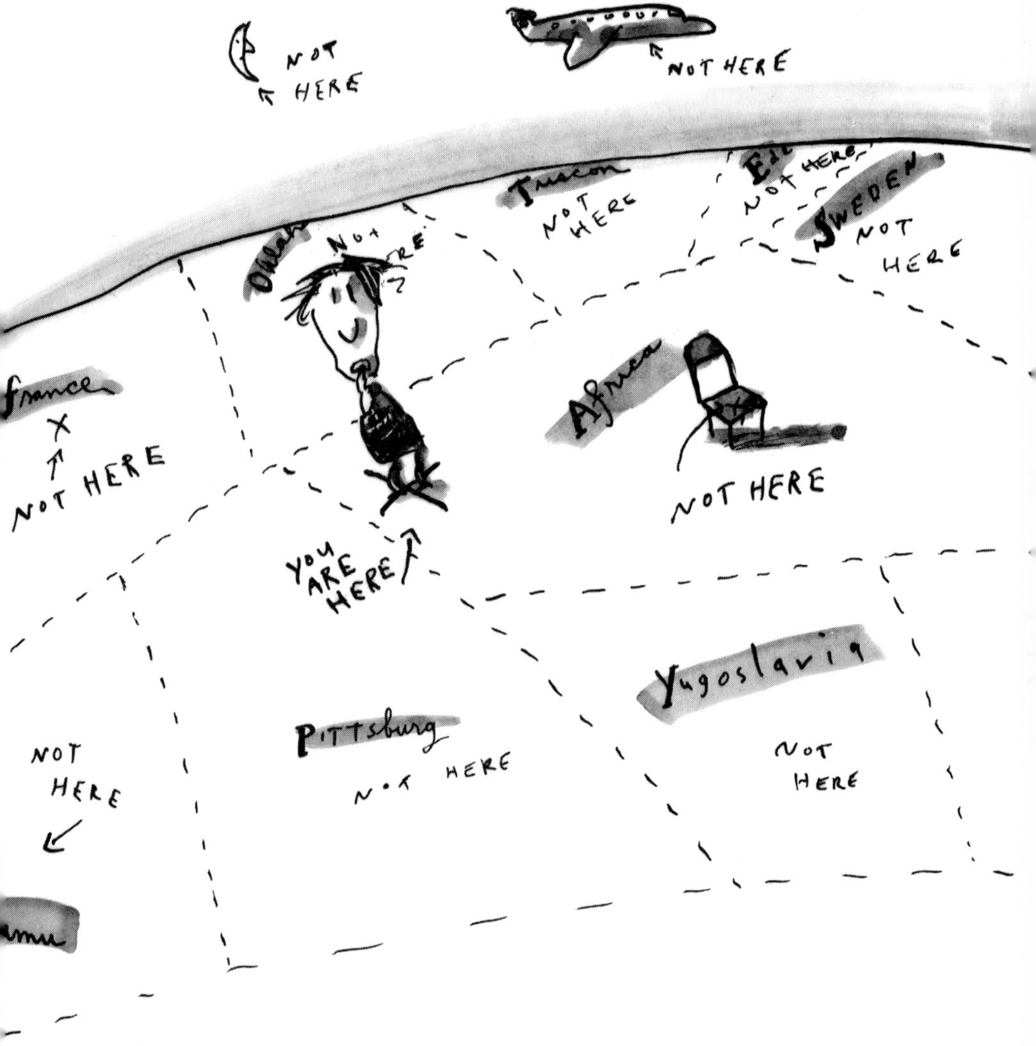

NOT HERE

NOT HERE

Tuscon NOT HERE

E... NOT HERE

SWEDEN NOT HERE

NOT HERE?

france ✗ NOT HERE

Africa NOT HERE

YOU ARE HERE ↗

NOT HERE ←

Pittsburg NOT HERE

Yugoslavia NOT HERE

...anm

Where am I?

Feeling a little disoriented

Things out there

Are we having fun yet?

Fear of Living

Her youth passed without distinction.

You are a dirty, worthless child

She had never boasted of either beauty or cleverness.

Her middle life was devoted to the care of a failing uncle,

and the endeavor to make a small income go a long way.

She had a home that wanted for nothing,

and was a great talker upon small matters.

Late in life she married a kind man in a pleasant civil ceremony;

within time they found they could communicate with few words.

Thinking herself
a happy and most
fortunate woman,

She died with
a song locked in
her heart.

Fear of dying

Remember: you SHOULD feel anxious.
There's a lot of thin ice
out there.

Bonnie Timmons lives with her husband, horses and cats in Philadelphia.

Before that she drew every day for The Denver Post.

Before that she worked for the Peace Corps in Kenya, which looked like this

Before that she dissected cadavers in Toronto, which looked like this:

Before that she won some ribbons for the 400 meter breast stroke in California which looked like this:

She always wanted to be either a ballerina or a baseball star.